Rhyme and Rhythm

The Green Book is the third book in the
Rhyme and Rhythm series.

Rhyme
and Rhythm

GREEN BOOK

Compiled by
J. GIBSON & R. WILSON

Illustrated by A. R. Whitear

MACMILLAN
London · Melbourne · Toronto

ST MARTIN'S PRESS
New York
1967

© J. Gibson & R. Wilson 1965

© Illustrations Macmillan & Co Ltd 1965
First Edition 1965
Reprinted 1966, 1967

MACMILLAN AND COMPANY LIMITED
Little Essex Street London WC2
also Bombay Calcutta Madras Melbourne

THE MACMILLAN COMPANY OF CANADA LIMITED
70 Bond Street Toronto 2

ST MARTIN'S PRESS INC
175 Fifth Avenue New York NY 10010

MADE AND PRINTED IN GREAT BRITAIN BY
WILLIAM CLOWES AND SONS, LIMITED, LONDON AND BECCLES

Contents

Acknowledgements

THE editors and publishers would like to thank the following, who have kindly given permission for the use of copyright material: Messrs. Basil Blackwell & Mott, Ltd., for 'Sir Nicketty Nox', by Hugh Chesterman; Mr. Kevin Crossley-Holland, for his translation of an Anglo-Saxon Riddle; Linda Davies, for 'Gipsy Dance'; the Literary Trustees of Walter de la Mare and the Society of Authors as their representative, for 'Nod'; Messrs. Gerald Duckworth & Co., Ltd., for 'George' and 'The Frog', from *Cautionary Verses*, by Hilaire Belloc; Miss Eleanor Farjeon and the Oxford University Press, for 'English', 'Nan' and 'The Waves of the Sea', from *The Children's Bells*; the Trustees of the Hardy Estate, for 'The Fallow Deer at the Lonely House', from *The Collected Poems of Thomas Hardy*; The Frederick Harris Music Co., Ltd., Ontario, for 'The Huron Carol', by J. Edgar Middleton; Mr. Ted Hughes and Messrs. Faber & Faber, Ltd., for 'My Brother Bert', from *Meet My Folks*; Mr. J. A. Lindon, for 'Sink Song'; Dr. John Masefield, O.M., and The Society of Authors, for 'Trade Winds'; Mr. Spike Milligan and Messrs. Dennis Dobson, for 'The Land of the Bumbley Boo', from *Silly Verse for Kids*; Mr. Ogden Nash, for 'The Tale of Custard the Dragon'; Messrs. Novello and Company, Ltd., for 'O No, John!', collected and arranged by Cecil Sharp; the Oxford University Press, for 'Kings Came Riding', by Charles Williams; Messrs. A. D. Peters & Co., for 'The End of the Road' and 'The Birds', by Hilaire Belloc; Mr. James Reeves and Messrs. William Heinemann, Ltd., for 'Jargon', from *Ragged Robin* and 'Mr. Tom Narrow' and 'Grim and Gloomy', from *The Wandering Moon*; Mr. Rudolf Sand and Messrs. J. M. Dent & Sons (Canada) Ltd., for 'Glorious it is', from *Anerca*, by Dr. Edmund Carpenter; Mr. Ian Serraillier and the Oxford University Press, for 'The Mouse in the Wainscot', from *The Tale of the Monster Horse*; Miss Margaret Stanley-Wrench, for 'Spring', and Mrs. Iris Wise, for 'The Snare', from *Collected Poems*, by James Stephens.

The editors would like to express their gratitude to the many schools and friends who have helped in the production of the books in the *Rhyme and Rhythm* series, either by their advice or by providing facilities for trying out the selections. They would like particularly to mention Mr. J. Beaumont and the staff of Wincheap Junior School, Canterbury, and Mr. R. Pollard and the staff of Christ Church Primary School, Folkestone; Mr. A. Lloyd Collins, Headmaster of the Perry Common Junior School, Birmingham, Miss Eleanor Smith, Headmistress of Galleywall J.M. School, Bermondsey, Mr. J. M. Thomas and Mr. Harley J. Usill, all of whom have been most generous in their help.

RECORD

Readers may like to know that a record of most of the poems and songs in this book has been made by Argo Record Company Limited. The serial number is RG 416.

COVER DESIGN AND RECORD SLEEVE

The editors and publishers are grateful to Robert Heath (aged 9) of Hollymount County Primary School, Wimbledon, whose painting was used in the design for the cover and the record sleeve.

Introduction

In compiling the four books of this anthology we have kept constantly in mind the readers for whom it is intended — children of from seven to eleven years of age. When selecting poems the anthologist can begin with pre-conceived and rigid principles about what poetry is and produce a selection narrow in its appeal, or go to the opposite extreme of trying to satisfy all tastes and produce a selection little better than a hotchpotch. We have tried to find a middle way by being as catholic in taste as we could be, while preserving such standards as are compatible with the genuine regard we have for the intelligence and discrimination of children in the Junior school.

We have first and foremost required of every poem admitted that it should both ring true and make a definite appeal in the class-room. In addition, we have attempted to provide both range and variety. You will find here regional poems alongside folk songs from America, bush songs from Australia, or translations from the Chinese; there are poems for every mood, from light-hearted jingles or limericks to tragic ballads and religious lyrics, poems familiar and unfamiliar, and poems by school-children as well as by great writers. If we have given little space to poems on fairyland, it is because we have found that the tone so often adopted by writers of this kind of verse is no longer acceptable to many children; instead we have favoured poetry that better expresses the wonder and excitement of our own age, and we are indebted to several contemporary poets who have written poems especially for this anthology. The words of songs have been included, where these have value in themselves, because we believe that the close relationship of music and poetry has often been blurred in the past and that children should be allowed to burst into song in the middle of a 'poetry' lesson if they wish to do so.

John Dryden once wrote that the chief end of poetry is delight. It is our sincere hope that RHYME AND RHYTHM will indeed be a source of delight, and that it will lead its readers to a lasting love of poetry.

Christ Church College
Canterbury

J.C.G.
R.W.

x

English

As gardens grow with flowers
English grows with words,
Words that have secret powers,
Words that give joy like birds.

Some of the words you say,
Both in and out of school,
Are brighter than the day,
And deeper than a pool.

Some words there are that dance,
Some words there are that sigh,
The fool's words come by chance,
The poet's to heaven fly.

When you are grown, your tongue
Should give the joy of birds;
Get while you are young
The gift of English words.

ELEANOR FARJEON

Jargon

Jerusalem, Joppa, Jericho —
These are the cities of long ago.

Jasper, jacinth, jet and jade —
Of such are jewels for ladies made.

Juniper's green and jasmine's white,
Sweet jonquil is spring's delight.

Joseph, Jeremy, Jennifer, James,
Julian, Juliet — just names.

January, July and June —
Birthday late or birthday soon.

Jacket, jersey, jerkin, jeans —
What's the wear for sweet sixteens?

Jaguar, jackal, jumbo, jay —
Came to dinner but couldn't stay.

Jellies, junkets, jumbals, jam —
Mix them up for sweet-toothed Sam.

To jig, to jaunt, to jostle, to jest —
These are the things that Jack loves best.

Jazz, jamboree, jubilee, joke —
The jolliest words you ever spoke.

From A to Z and Z to A
The joyfullest letter of all is J.

JAMES REEVES

As

As wet as a fish — as dry as a bone;
As live as a bird — as dead as a stone;
As plump as a partridge — as poor as a rat;
As strong as a horse — as weak as a cat;
As hard as flint — as soft as a mole;
As white as a lily — as black as coal;
As plain as a pike-staff — as rough as a bear;
As tight as a drum — as free as the air;
As heavy as lead — as light as a feather;
As steady as time — uncertain as weather;
As hot as a furnace — as cold as a frog;
As gay as a lark — as sick as a dog;
As slow as a tortoise — as swift as the wind;
As true as the gospel — as false as mankind;
As thin as a herring — as fat as a pig;
As proud as a peacock — as blithe as a grig;
As fierce as a tiger — as mild as a dove;
As stiff as a poker — as limp as a glove;
As blind as a bat — as deaf as a post;
As cool as a cucumber — as warm as toast;
As flat as a flounder — as round as a ball;
As blunt as a hammer — as sharp as an awl;
As red as a ferret — as safe as the stocks;
As bold as a thief — as sly as a fox;
As straight as an arrow — as bent as a bow;
As yellow as saffron — as black as a sloe;
As brittle as glass — as tough as gristle;
As neat as my nail — as clean as a whistle;

3

As good as a feast — as bad as a witch;
As light as is day — as dark as is pitch;
As brisk as a bee — as dull as an ass;
As full as a tick — as solid as brass.

UNKNOWN

O No, John!

'On yonder hill there stands a creature;
Who she is I do not know.
I'll go and court her for her beauty;
She must answer Yes or No.'
    'O No, John! No, John! No, John! No!

'My father was a Spanish Captain,
Went to sea a month ago.
First he kissed me, then he left me,
Bid me always answer No.
    O No, John! No, John! No, John! No!'

'O madam, in your face is beauty,
On your lips red roses grow.
Will you take me for your lover?
Madam, answer Yes or No.'
    'O No, John! No, John! No, John! No!'

'O madam, I will give you jewels;
I will make you rich and free;
I will give you silken dresses.
Madam, will you marry me?'
    'O No, John! No, John! No, John! No!'

4

'O madam, since you are so cruel,
And that you do scorn me so,
If I may not be your lover,
Madam, will you let me go?'
　　'O No, John! No, John! No, John! No!'

'Then I will stay with you for ever,
If you will not be unkind,
Madam, I have vowed to love you;
Would you have me change my mind?'
　　'O No, John! No, John! No, John! No!'

'O hark! I hear the church bells ringing:
Will you come and be my wife?
Or, dear madam, have you settled
To live single all your life?'
　　'O No, John! No, John! No, John! No!'

FOLK SONG

5

The Lady of Shalott

PART I

On either side the river lie
Long fields of barley and of rye,
That clothe the wold and meet the sky;
And thro' the field the road runs by
    To many-tower'd Camelot;
And up and down the people go,
Gazing where the lilies blow
Round an island there below,
    The island of Shalott.

Willows whiten, aspens quiver,
Little breezes dusk and shiver
Thro' the wave that runs for ever
By the island in the river
    Flowing down to Camelot.
Four grey walls, and four grey towers,
Overlook a space of flowers,
And the silent isle imbowers
    The Lady of Shalott.

By the margin, willow-veil'd,
Slide the heavy barges trail'd
By slow horses; and unhail'd
The shallop flitteth silken-sail'd
    Skimming down to Camelot:

But who hath seen her wave her hand?
Or at the casement seen her stand?
Or is she known in all the land,
     The Lady of Shalott?

Only reapers, reaping early
In among the bearded barley,
Hear a song that echoes cheerly
From the river winding clearly,
     Down to tower'd Camelot:
And by the moon the reaper weary,
Piling sheaves in uplands airy,
Listening, whispers ' 'Tis the fairy
     Lady of Shalott.'

PART II

There she weaves by night and day
A magic web with colours gay.
She has heard a whisper say,
A curse is on her if she stay
     To look down to Camelot.
She knows not what the curse may be,
And so she weaveth steadily,
And little other care hath she,
     The Lady of Shalott.

And moving thro' a mirror clear
That hangs before her all the year,
Shadows of the world appear.
There she sees the highway near
  Winding down to Camelot:
There the river eddy whirls,
And there the surly village-churls,
And the red cloaks of market girls,
  Pass onward from Shalott.

Sometimes a troop of damsels glad,
An abbot on an ambling pad,
Sometimes a curly shepherd-lad,
Or long-hair'd page in crimson clad
  Goes by to tower'd Camelot;
And sometimes thro' the mirror blue
The knights come riding two and two:
She hath no loyal knight and true,
  The Lady of Shalott.

But in her web she still delights
To weave the mirror's magic sights,
For often thro' the silent nights
A funeral, with plumes and lights
  And music, went to Camelot:
Or when the moon was overhead,
Came two young lovers lately wed;
'I am half sick of shadows,' said
  The Lady of Shalott.

PART III

A bow-shot from her bower-eaves,
He rode between the barley-sheaves,
The sun came dazzling thro' the leaves,
And flamed upon the brazen greaves
  Of bold Sir Lancelot.
A red-cross knight for ever kneel'd
To a lady in his shield,
That sparkled on the yellow field,
  Beside remote Shalott.

The gemmy bridle glitter'd free,
Like to some branch of stars we see
Hung in the golden Galaxy.
The bridle bells rang merrily
  As he rode down to Camelot:
And from his blazon'd baldric slung
A mighty silver bugle hung,
And as he rode his armour rung,
  Beside remote Shalott.

All in the blue unclouded weather
Thick-jewell'd shone the saddle leather,
The helmet and the helmet-feather
Burn'd like one burning flame together,
  As he rode down to Camelot.
As often thro' the purple night,
Below the starry clusters bright,
Some bearded meteor, trailing light,
  Moves over still Shalott.

9

His broad clear brow in sunlight glow'd;
On burnish'd hooves his war-horse trode;
From underneath his helmet flow'd
His coal-black curls as on he rode,
    As he rode down to Camelot.
From the bank and from the river
He flash'd into the crystal mirror,
'Tirra lirra,' by the river
    Sang Sir Lancelot.

She left the web, she left the loom,
She made three paces thro' the room,
She saw the water-lily bloom,
She saw the helmet and the plume,
    She look'd down to Camelot.
Out flew the web and floated wide;
The mirror crack'd from side to side;
'The curse is come upon me,' cried
    The Lady of Shalott.

PART IV

In the stormy east-wind straining,
The pale yellow woods were waning,
The broad stream in his banks complaining,
Heavily the low sky raining
    Over tower'd Camelot;

Down she came and found a boat
Beneath a willow left afloat,
And round about the prow she wrote
   The Lady of Shalott.

And down the river's dim expanse —
Like some bold seër in a trance,
Seeing all his own mischance —
With a glassy countenance
   Did she look to Camelot.
And at the closing of the day
She loosed the chain, and down she lay;
The broad stream bore her far away,
   The Lady of Shalott.

Lying, robed in snowy white
That loosely flew to left and right —
The leaves upon her falling light —
Thro' the noises of the night
   She floated down to Camelot:
And as the boat-head wound along
The willowy hills and fields among,
They heard her singing her last song,
   The Lady of Shalott.

Heard a carol, mournful, holy,
Chanted loudly, chanted lowly,
Till her blood was frozen slowly,
And her eyes were darken'd wholly,
   Turn'd to tower'd Camelot;

For ere she reach'd upon the tide
The first house by the water-side,
Singing in her song she died,
    The Lady of Shalott.

Under tower and balcony,
By garden-wall and gallery,
A gleaming shape she floated by,
Dead-pale between the houses high,
    Silent into Camelot.
Out upon the wharfs they came,
Knight and burgher, lord and dame,
And round the prow they read her name,
    The Lady of Shalott.

Who is this? and what is here?
And in the lighted palace near
Died the sound of royal cheer;
And they cross'd themselves for fear,
    All the knights at Camelot:
But Lancelot mused a little space;
He said, 'She has a lovely face;
God in His mercy lend her grace,
    The Lady of Shalott.'

LORD TENNYSON

Earl Haldan's Daughter

It was Earl Haldan's daughter,
　She looked across the sea;
She looked across the water,
　And long and loud laughed she.
'The locks of six princesses
　Must be my marriage fee,
So hey bonny boat, and ho bonny boat!
　Who comes a-wooing me?'

It was Earl Haldan's daughter,
　And she walked along the strand;
When she was aware of a knight so fair,
　Come sailing to the land.
His sails were all of velvet,
　His masts of beaten gold,
And hey bonny boat, and ho bonny boat!
　Who saileth here so bold?

'The locks of five princesses
　I won beyond the sea;
I clipt their golden tresses,
　To fringe a cloak for thee.
One handful yet is wanting,
　But one of all the tale;
So hey bonny boat, and ho bonny boat!
　Furl up thy velvet sail!'

He leapt into the water,
    That rover young and bold;
He gript Earl Haldan's daughter,
    He clipt her locks of gold;
'Go weep, go weep, proud maiden,
    The tale is full today.
Now hey bonny boat, and ho bonny boat!
    Sail westward ho away!'

CHARLES KINGSLEY

A Royal Wedding

A Princess, proud and beautiful,
    When she was seventeen
Declared that she'd be dutiful
    To please the King and Queen:
'I'll marry an Emperor,' she said,
'If he's rich and famous and not dead.'

The Emperors flocked by sea and land
    And fell upon their knees,
Each shouting she should take his hand,
    But still they failed to please.
'I'll marry none of them,' she said,
'For I think they're wretchedly ill-bred.'

The Princess still was not a bride
    Though she was twenty-four
(For love of her two Kings had died
    And Earls and Dukes galore);

'Since the Commons want me to,' said she,
'I'll marry a Prince, if needs must be.'

So Princes by the dozen sped
      From north, south, east and west:
Each one was handsome, tall, well-bred,
      And wore his Sunday-best.
'It's funny how new faces strike you,'
The Princess said, 'but I just don't like you!'

This was enough to be downcast by
      It's only fair to say,
And while the next two decades passed by
      Her beauty passed away,
Till no one at all was left to sweethéart her —
Not so much as a Knight of the Garter.

When she grew ugly-old at last
      With not a tooth in her head
How sorry she was for the time gone past,
      How sorry she had not wed!
'If I'd known I'd die an old maid,' she cried,
'I'd have married a Duke and swallowed my pride.'

But Fate felt sorry to see cry
      A Princess once so pretty
And soon a beggarman came by
      Who looked at her with pity.
'If Your Highness gives me her fortune,' he said....
And Her Highness did, and so she was wed!

RAYMOND WILSON

Nan

It's
    Nan! Nan! where have you got to?
    Nan? Nan? you know it's not right!
    Now then, you *are* to! Now then, you're *not* to!
    That's how it is from morning to night.

    Just whatever you've set your heart on
    They put a stop to, I don't know why.
    There's a new black calf been born in the barton,
    And ten pigwiggins in Grunter's sty —

But it's
    Nan! Nan! where are you going?
    Nan! Nan! where have you been?
    And the game is up if they know you're knowing
    Who is calling and what they mean.

    There's a pheasant's clutch hid under the bracken,
    And Tib's got her kittens behind the shed,
    Two grey tabbies, a white-and-black 'un,
    A tortoise-shell, and a gold-and-red.

And it's
   Nan! Nan! what are you doing?
   Nan! Nan! what have you done?
   Then you know there is trouble brewing,
   And you stop your ears and begin to run.

   There's newts in the ditch below the alder,
   And a squirrel's nest in the round-oak tree —
   You never saw bulgier eyes or balder
   Babies than squirrel's baby-three.

Then it's
   Turn your frock? (Huh! it's only cotton!)
   Look at your hands! you *are* a sight! —
   They've simply forgotten. They've simply
            forgotten,
   And that's how it is from morning to night.

                              ELEANOR FARJEON

Mr Tom Narrow

   A scandalous man
      Was Mr Tom Narrow,
   He pushed his grandmother
      Round in a barrow.
   And he called out loud
      As he rang his bell,
   'Grannies to sell!
      Old grannies to sell!'

The neighbours said,
 As he passed them by,
'This poor old lady
 We will not buy.
He surely must be
 A mischievous man
To try for to sell
 His own dear Gran!'

'Besides,' said another,
 'If you ask me,
She'd be very small use
 That I can see.'
'You're right,' said a third,
 'And no mistake —
A very poor bargain
 She'd surely make.'

So Mr Tom Narrow,
 He scratched his head,
And he sent his grandmother
 Back to bed;
And he rang his bell
 Through all the town
Till he sold his barrow
 For half a crown.

JAMES REEVES

Sir Nicketty Nox

Sir Nicketty Nox was an ancient knight,
  So old was he that he'd lost his sight.
Blind as a mole, and slim as a fox,
  And dry as a stick was Sir Nicketty Nox.

His sword and buckler were old and cracked,
  So was his charger and that's a fact.
Thin as a rake from head to hocks,
  Was this rickety nag of Sir Nicketty Nox.

A wife he had and daughters three,
  And all were as old as old could be.
They mended the shirts and darned the socks
  Of that old antiquity, Nicketty Nox.

Sir Nicketty Nox would fly in a rage
  If anyone tried to guess his age.
He'd mouth and mutter and tear his locks,
  This very pernickety Nicketty Nox.

HUGH CHESTERMAN

Soldier, Soldier

'Oh! Soldier, soldier, won't you marry me,
  With your musket, fife and drum?'
'Oh no, sweet maid, I cannot marry thee,
  For I have no coat to put on.'

So up she went to her grandfather's chest,
And she got him a coat of the very, very best
  And the soldier put it on!

'Oh! Soldier, soldier, won't you marry me,
  With your musket, fife and drum?'
'Oh no, sweet maid, I cannot marry thee,
  For I have no hat to put on.'

So up she went to her grandfather's chest,
And she got him a hat of the very, very best,
  And the soldier put it on!

'Oh! Soldier, soldier, won't you marry me,
  With your musket, fife and drum?'
'Oh no, sweet maid, I cannot marry thee,
  For I have no boots to put on.'

So up she went to her grandfather's chest,
And she got him a pair of the very, very best,
  And the soldier put them on!

'Oh! Soldier, soldier, won't you marry me,
  With your musket, fife and drum?'
Oh no, sweet maid, I cannot marry thee,
  For I have a wife of my own!'

FOLK SONG

George

Who played with a Dangerous Toy, and suffered a Catastrophe of considerable Dimensions.

When George's Grandmamma was told
That George had been as good as Gold,
She Promised in the Afternoon
To buy him an *Immense* BALLOON.

And so she did; but when it came,
It got into the candle flame,
And being of a dangerous sort
Exploded with a loud report!

The Lights went out! The Windows broke!
The Room was filled with reeking smoke.
And in the darkness shrieks and yells
Were mingled with Electric Bells,
And falling masonry and groans,
And crunching, as of broken bones,
And dreadful shrieks, when, worst of all,
The House itself began to fall!
It tottered, shuddering to and fro,
Then crashed into the street below —
Which happened to be Savile Row.

When help arrived, among the Dead
Were Cousin Mary, Little Fred,
The Footmen (both of them), the Groom,
The man that cleaned the Billiard-Room,
The Chaplain, and the Still-Room Maid.

And I am dreadfully afraid
That Monsieur Champignon, the Chef,
Will now be permanently deaf —
And both his Aides are much the same;
While George, who was in part to blame,
Received, you will regret to hear,
A nasty lump behind the ear.

Moral

The moral is that little Boys
Should not be given dangerous Toys.

HILAIRE BELLOC

My Brother Bert

Pets are the Hobby of my brother Bert.
He used to go to school with a Mouse in his shirt.

His Hobby it grew, as some hobbies will,
And grew and GREW and GREW until —

Oh don't breathe a word, pretend you haven't
     heard.
A simply appalling thing has occurred —

The very thought makes me iller and iller:
Bert's brought home a gigantic Gorilla!

If you think that's really not such a scare,
What if it quarrels with his Grizzly Bear?

You still think you could keep your head?
What if the Lion from under the bed

And the four Ostriches that deposit
Their football eggs in his bedroom closet

And the Aardvark out of his bottom drawer
All danced out and joined in the Roar?

What if the Pangolins were to caper
Out of their nests behind the wallpaper?

With the fifty sorts of Bats
That hang on his hatstand like old hats,

And out of a shoebox the excitable Platypus
Along with the Ocelot or Jungle-Cattypus?

The Wombat, the Dingo, the Gecko,
          the Grampus —
How they would shake the house with their
          Rumpus!

Not to forget the Bandicoot
Who would certainly peer from his battered old
          boot.

Why it would be a dreadful day,
And what Oh what would the neighbours say!

TED HUGHES

Kilkenny Cats

There once were two cats of Kilkenny
Each thought there was one cat too many;
So they fought and they fit,
And they scratched and they bit,
Till, excepting their nails
And the tips of their tails,
Instead of two cats there weren't any.

UNKNOWN

The Tale of Custard
the Dragon

Belinda lived in a little white house,
With a little black kitten and a little grey mouse,
And a little yellow dog and a little red wagon,
And a realio, trulio, little pet dragon.

Now the name of the little black kitten was Ink,
And the little grey mouse, she called her Blink,
And the little yellow dog was sharp as Mustard,
But the dragon was a coward, and she called him
       Custard.

Custard the dragon had big sharp teeth,
And spikes on top of him and scales underneath,
Mouth like a fireplace, chimney for a nose,
And realio, trulio daggers on his toes.

Belinda was as brave as a barrelful of bears,
And Ink and Blink chased lions down the stairs,
Mustard was as brave as a tiger in a rage,
But Custard cried for a nice safe cage.

Belinda tickled him, she tickled him unmerciful,
Ink, Blink and Mustard, they rudely called him Percival,
They all sat laughing in the little red wagon
At the realio, trulio, cowardly dragon.

Belinda giggled till she shook the house,
And Blink said *Weeek!*, which is giggling for a mouse,
Ink and Mustard rudely asked his age,
When Custard cried for a nice safe cage.

Suddenly, suddenly they heard a nasty sound,
And Mustard growled, and they all looked around.
Meowch! cried Ink, and Ooh! cried Belinda,
For there was a pirate, climbing in the winda.

Pistol in his left hand, pistol in his right,
And he held in his teeth a cutlass bright;
His beard was black, one leg was wood.
It was clear that the pirate meant no good.

Belinda paled, and she cried Help! Help!
But Mustard fled with a terrified yelp,
Ink trickled down to the bottom of the household,
And little mouse Blink strategically mouseholed.

But up jumped Custard, snorting like an engine,
Clashed his tail like irons in a dungeon,
With a clatter and a clank and a jangling squirm
He went at the pirate like a robin at a worm.

The pirate gaped at Belinda's dragon,
And gulped some grog from his pocket flagon,
He fired two bullets, but they didn't hit,
And Custard gobbled him, every bit.

Belinda embraced him, Mustard licked him;
No one mourned for his pirate victim.
Ink and Blink in glee did gyrate
Around the dragon that ate the pyrate.

Belinda still lives in her little white house,
With her little black kitten and her little grey mouse,
And her little yellow dog and her little red wagon,
And her realio, trulio, little pet dragon.

Belinda is as brave as a barrelful of bears,
And Ink and Blink chase lions down the stairs,
Mustard is as brave as a tiger in a rage,
But Custard keeps crying for a nice safe cage.

OGDEN NASH

The Frog

Be kind and tender to the Frog,
And do not call him names,
As 'Slimy skin', or 'Polly-wog',
Or otherwise 'Ugly James',
Or 'Gap-a-grin', or 'Toad-gone-wrong',
Or 'Billy Bandy-knees'.
The Frog is justly sensitive
To epithets like these.
No animal will more repay
A treatment kind and fair;
At least so lonely people say
Who keep a frog (and, by the way,
They are extremely rare).

HILAIRE BELLOC

The Mouse in the Wainscot

Hush, Suzanne!
Don't lift your cup.
That breath you heard
Is a mouse getting up.

As the mist that steams
From your milk as you sup,
So soft is the sound
Of a mouse getting up.

There! did you hear
His feet pitter-patter,
Lighter than tipping
Of beads in a platter,

And then like a shower
On the window pane
The little feet scampering
Back again?

O falling of feather!
O drift of a leaf!
The mouse in the wainscot
Is dropping asleep.

IAN SERRAILLIER

The Plaint of the Camel

Canary-birds feed on sugar and seed,
    Parrots have crackers to crunch;
And as for the poodles, they tell me the noodles
    Have chicken and cream for their lunch.
But there's never a question
About MY digestion,
    ANYTHING does for me.

Cats, you're aware, can repose in a chair,
    Chickens can roost upon rails;

Puppies are able to sleep in a stable,
   And oysters can slumber in pails.
But no-one supposes
A poor camel dozes.
   ANY PLACE does for me.

      Lambs are enclosed where it's never exposed,
         Coops are constructed for hens;
      Kittens are treated to houses well heated,
         And pigs are protected by pens.
      But a camel comes handy
      Wherever it's sandy,
         ANYWHERE does for me.

People would laugh if you rode a giraffe,
   Or mounted the back of an ox;
It's nobody's habit to ride on a rabbit,
   Or try to bestraddle a fox.
But as for a camel, he's
Ridden by families —
   ANY LOAD does for me.

      A snake is as round as a hole in the ground;
         Weasels are wavy and sleek;
      And no alligator could ever be straighter
         Than lizards that live in a creek.
      But a camel's all lumpy,
      And bumpy, and humpy,
         ANY SHAPE does for me.

                              CHARLES EDWARD CARRYL

Sink Song

Scouring out the porridge pot,
　　Round and round and round!

　　　Out with all the scraith and scoopery.
　　　Lift the eely ooly droopery,
　　　Chase the glubbery slubbery gloopery
　　　　Round and round and round!

　　　Out with all the doleful dithery,
　　　Ladle out the slimery slithery,
　　　Hunt and catch the hithery thithery,
　　　　Round and round and round!

　　　Out with all the obbly gubbly,
　　　On the stove it burns so bubbly,
　　　Use the spoon and use it doubly,
　　　　Round and round and round!

J. A. LINDON

A Limerick

A diner while dining at Crewe
Found quite a large mouse in his stew.
　　Said the waiter, 'Don't shout
　　And wave it about,
Or the rest will be wanting one, too!'

UNKNOWN

And Another

There was a young farmer of Leeds
Who swallowed six packets of seeds.
   It soon came to pass
   He was covered with grass,
And he couldn't sit down for the weeds.

UNKNOWN

And Another

There once was a lady of Riga
Who went for a ride on a tiger.
   They returned from the ride
   With the lady inside
And a smile on the face of the tiger.

UNKNOWN

The Land of the Bumbley Boo

In the Land of the Bumbley Boo
The people are red white and blue,
   They never blow noses,
   Or ever wear closes;
What a sensible thing to do!

In the Land of the Bumbley Boo
You can buy Lemon pie at the Zoo;
They give away Foxes
In little Pink Boxes
And Bottles of Dandelion Stew.

In the Land of the Bumbley Boo
You never see a Gnu,
But thousands of cats
Wearing trousers and hats
Made of Pumpkins and Pelican Glue!

Oh, the Bumbley Boo! the Bumbley Boo!
That's the place for me and you!
So hurry! Let's run!
The train leaves at one!
For the Land of the Bumbley Boo!
The wonderful Bumbley Boo-Boo-Boo!
The Wonderful Bumbley BOO!!!

SPIKE MILLIGAN

Grim and Gloomy

Oh, grim and gloomy,
So grim and gloomy
Are the caves beneath the sea.
Oh, rare but roomy
And bare and boomy,
Those salt sea caverns be.

Oh, slim and slimy
Or grey and grimy
Are the animals of the sea.
Salt and oozy
And safe and snoozy
The caves where those animals be.

Hark to the shuffling,
Huge and snuffling,
Ravenous, cavernous, great sea-beasts!
But fair and fabulous,
Tintinnabulous,
Gay and fabulous are their feasts.

Ah, but the queen of the sea,
The querulous, perilous sea!
How the curls of her tresses
The pearls on her dresses,
Sway and swirl in the waves,
How cosy and dozy,
How sweet ring-a-rosy
Her bower in the deep-sea caves!

Oh, rare but roomy
And bare and boomy
Those caverns under the sea,
And grave and grandiose,
Safe and sandiose
The dens of her denizens be.

JAMES REEVES

The Death of Admiral Benbow

Come all you seamen bold and draw near, and draw near,
Come all you seamen bold and draw near.
It's of an admiral's fame, O brave Benbow was his name,
How he fought all on the main you shall hear, you shall
     hear.

Brave Benbow he set sail for to fight, for to fight,
Brave Benbow he set sail for to fight;
Brave Benbow he set sail with a fine and pleasant gale,
But his captains they turned tail in a fright, in a fright.

Says Kirby unto Wade, we will run, we will run,
Says Kirby unto Wade, we will run;
For I value no disgrace, nor the losing of my place,
But the enemy I won't face nor his guns, nor his guns.

The Ruby and Benbow fought the French, fought the
     French,
The Ruby and Benbow fought the French;
They fought them up and down, till the blood came
     trickling down,
Till the blood came trickling down where they lay,
     where they lay.

Brave Benbow lost his legs by chain-shot, by chain-shot,
Brave Benbow lost his legs by chain-shot;
Brave Benbow lost his legs, and all on his stumps he begs —
Fight on, my English lads, 'tis our lot, 'tis our lot.

The surgeon dressed his wounds; cries Benbow, cries
    Benbow;
The Surgeon dressed his wounds; cries Benbow —
Let a cradle now in haste on the quarter deck be placed,
That the enemy I may face till I die, till I die.

'Twas on Tuesday morning last Benbow died, Benbow
    died,
'Twas on Tuesday morning last Benbow died:
What a shocking sight to see brave Benbow carried away,
He was buried in Kingston church, there he lay, there he lay.

UNKNOWN

The End of the Road

In these boots and with this staff
Two hundred leaguers and a half
Walked I, went I, paced I, tripped I,
Marched I, held I, skelped I, slipped I,
Pushed I, panted, swung and dashed I;
Picked I, forded, swam and splashed I,
Strolled I, climbed I, crawled and scrambled,
Dropped and dipped I, ranged and rambled;
Plodded I, hobbled I, trudged and tramped I,
And in lonely spinnies camped I,
Lingered, loitered, limped and crept I,
Clambered, halted, stepped and leapt I,
Slowly sauntered, roundly strode I,
    And...
    Let me not conceal it...rode I.

HILAIRE BELLOC

The American Railway

In eighteen hundred and eighty-one
The American Railway was begun,
In eighteen hundred and eighty-one,
Working on the railway.

In eighteen hundred and eighty-two
I found myself with nothing to do,
In eighteen hundred and eighty-two,
But work upon the railway.

In eighteen hundred and eighty-three
The overseer accepted me,
In eighteen hundred and eighty-three,
To work upon the railway.

In eighteen hundred and eighty-four
My hands were tired and my feet were sore,
In eighteen hundred and eighty-four,
With working on the railway.

In eighteen hundred and eighty-five
I found myself more dead than alive,
In eighteen hundred and eighty-five,
Through working on the railway.

In eighteen hundred and eighty-six
I trod on a box of dynamite sticks,
In eighteen hundred and eighty-six,
Working on the railway.

In eighteen hundred and eighty-seven
I found myself on the way to heaven,
In eighteen hundred and eighty-seven,
Working on the railway.

In eighteen hundred and eighty-eight
I found myself at the Golden Gate,
In eighteen hundred and eighty-eight,
Working on the railway.

In eighteen hundred and eighty-nine
A cherub's harp and wings were mine,
In eighteen hundred and eighty-nine
Above the American railway.

In eighteen hundred and eighty-ten
If you want any more we will sing it again,
In eighteen hundred and eighty-ten,
Working on the railway.

UNKNOWN

The White-Footed Deer

It was a hundred years ago,
  When, by the woodland ways,
The traveller saw the wild deer drink,
  Or crop the birchen sprays.

Beneath a hill, whose rocky side
  O'erbrowed a grassy mead,
And fenced a cottage from the wind,
  A deer was wont to feed.

She only came when on the cliffs
  The evening moonlight lay,
And no man knew the secret haunts
  In which she walked by day.

White were her feet, her forehead showed
  A spot of silvery white,
That seemed to glimmer like a star
  In autumn's hazy night.

And here, when sang the whippoorwill,
  She cropped the sprouting leaves,
And here her rustling steps were heard
  On still October eves.

But when the broad midsummer moon
  Rose o'er that grassy lawn,
Beside the silver-footed deer
  There grazed a spotted fawn.

The cottage dame forbade her son
  To aim the rifle here;
'It were a sin,' she said, 'to harm
  Or fright that friendly deer.

'This spot has been my pleasant home
    Ten peaceful years and more;
And ever when the moonlight shines,
    She feeds before our door.

'The red men say that here she walked
    A thousand moons ago;
They never raise the war-whoop here,
    And never twang the bow.

'I love to watch her as she feeds,
    And think that all is well,
While such a gentle creature haunts
    The place in which we dwell.'

The youth obeyed, and sought for game
    In forests far away,
Where deep in silence and in moss,
    The ancient woodland lay.

But once, in autumn's golden time,
    He ranged the wild in vain,
Nor roused the pheasant nor the deer,
    And wandered home again.

The crescent moon and crimson eve
    Shone with a mingling light;
The deer upon the grassy mead
    Was feeding full in sight.

He raised the rifle to his eye,
    And from the cliffs around
A sudden echo, shrill and sharp,
    Gave back its deadly sound.

Away into the neighbouring wood
    The startled creature flew,
And crimson drops at morning lay
    Amid the glimmering dew.

Next evening shone the waxing moon
    As sweetly as before;
The deer upon the grassy mead
    Was seen again no more.

But ere that crescent moon was old
    By night the red men came,
And burnt the cottage to the ground,
    And slew the youth and dame.

Now woods have overgrown the mead,
    And hid the cliffs from sight;
There shrieks the hovering hawk at noon,
    And prowls the fox at night.

WILLIAM CULLEN BRYANT

Meeting

As I went home on the old wood road,
  With my basket and lesson book,
A deer came out of the tall trees
  And down to drink at the brook.

Twilight was all about us,
  Twilight and tree on tree;
I looked straight into its great, strange eyes,
  And the deer looked back at me.

Beautiful, brown, and unafraid,
  Those eyes returned my stare;
And something with neither sound nor name
  Passed between us there.

Something I shall not forget —
  Something still, and shy, and wise —
In the dimness of the woods
  From a pair of gold-flecked eyes.

RACHEL FIELD

The Fallow Deer at the Lonely House

One without looks in tonight
    Through the curtain-chink
From the sheet of glistening white;
One without looks in tonight
    As we sit and think
    By the fender-brink.

We do not discern those eyes
    Watching in the snow;
Lit by lamps of rosy dyes
We do not discern those eyes
    Wondering, aglow,
    Fourfooted, tiptoe.

THOMAS HARDY

My Heart's in the Highlands

My heart's in the Highlands, my heart is not here;
My heart's in the Highlands, a-chasing the deer;
Chasing the wild deer, and following the roe —
My heart's in the Highlands wherever I go.
    Farewell to the Highlands, farewell to the North!
    The birthplace of valour, the country of worth;
    Wherever I wander, wherever I rove,
    The hills of the Highlands for ever I love.

Farewell to the mountains high covered with snow!
Farewell to the straths and green valleys below!
Farewell to the forests and wild-hanging woods!
Farewell to the torrents and loud-pouring floods!
My heart's in the Highlands, my heart is not here,
My heart's in the Highlands, a-chasing the deer;
Chasing the wild deer, and following the roe —
My heart's in the Highlands wherever I go.

ROBERT BURNS

Glorious it is

Glorious it is to see
The caribou flocking down from the forests
And beginning
Their wanderings to the north.
Timidly they watch
For the pitfalls of man.
Glorious it is to see
The great herds from the forests
Spreading out over plains of white.

Glorious it is to see
Early summer's short-haired caribou
Beginning to wander.
Glorious to see them trot
To and fro
Across the promontories,
Seeking for a crossing place.

Glorious it is
To see great musk oxen
Gathering in herds.
The little dogs they watch for
When they gather in herds.
Glorious to see.

Glorious it is
To see the long-haired winter caribou
Returning to the forests.
Fearfully they watch
For the little people,
While the herd follows the ebb-mark of the sea
With a storm of clattering hooves.
Glorious it is
When wandering time is come.

Eskimo Poem (translated by
DR EDMUND CARPENTER)

The Piper

Piping down the valleys wild,
    Piping songs of pleasant glee,
On a cloud I saw a child,
    And he laughing said to me:

'Pipe a song about a lamb!'
    So I piped with merry cheer.
'Piper, pipe that song again.'
    So I piped: he wept to hear.

'Drop thy pipe, thy happy pipe;
  Sing thy song of happy cheer!'
So I sang the same again,
  While he wept with joy to hear.

'Piper sit thee down and write
  In a book that all may read.'
So he vanished from my sight;
  And I plucked a hollow reed,

And I made a rural pen,
  And I stained the water clear,
And I wrote my happy songs,
  Every child may joy to hear.

WILLIAM BLAKE

The Piper

A piper in the streets today
Set up and tuned, and started to play,
And away, away, away on the tide
Of his music we started; on every side
Doors and windows were opened wide,
And men left their work and came,
And women with petticoats coloured like flame,
And little bare feet that were blue with cold,
Went dancing back to the age of gold,
And all the world went gay, went gay,
For half an hour in the street today.

SEUMAS O'SULLIVAN

The Chimney
Sweeper

When my mother died I was very young,
And my father sold me while yet my tongue
Could scarcely cry ' 'weep! 'weep! 'weep!'
So your chimneys I sweep, and in soot I sleep.

There's little Tom Dacre, who cried when his head,
That curled like a lamb's back, was shaved: so I said,
'Hush, Tom! never mind it, for when your head's bare
You know that the soot cannot spoil your white hair.'

And so he was quiet, and that very night,
As Tom was a-sleeping, he had such a sight!
That thousands of sweepers, Dick, Joe, Ned, and Jack,
Were all of them locked up in coffins of black.

And by came an Angel who had a bright key,
And he opened the coffins and set them all free;
Then down a green plain leaping, laughing they run,
And wash in a river, and shine in the Sun.

Then naked and white, all their bags left behind,
They rise upon clouds and sport in the wind;
And the Angel told Tom, if he'd be a good boy,
He'd have God for his father, and never want joy.

And so Tom awoke; and we rose in the dark,
And got with our bags and our brushes to work.
Tho' the morning was cold, Tom was happy and
warm;
So if all do their duty they need not fear harm.

WILLIAM BLAKE

A Warning

The robin and the redbreast,
    The robin and the wren,
If you take them out of their nest,
    Ye'll ne'er thrive again.

The robin and the redbreast,
    The martin and the swallow,
If you touch one of their eggs,
    Ill luck is sure to follow.

UNKNOWN

Little Trotty Wagtail

Little trotty wagtail, he went in the rain,
And twittering, tottering sideways he ne'er got straight
    again.
He stooped to get a worm, and looked up to get a fly,
And then he flew away ere his feathers they were dry.

Little trotty wagtail, he waddled in the mud,
And left his little footmarks, trample where he would.
He waddled in the water-pudge, and waggle went his tail,
And chirruped up his wings to dry upon the garden rail.

Little trotty wagtail, you nimble all about,
And in the dimpling water-pudge you waddle in and out;
Your home is nigh at hand, and in the warm pig-sty,
So, little Master Wagtail, I'll bid you a good-bye.

JOHN CLARE

Birds' Nests

The skylark's nest among the grass
And waving corn is found;
The robin's on a shady bank,
With oak leaves strewn around.

The wren builds in an ivied thorn,
Or old and ruined wall;
The mossy nest, so covered in,
You scarce can see at all.

The martins build their nests of clay,
In rows beneath the eaves;
While silvery lichens, moss and hair,
The chaffinch interweaves.

The cuckoo makes no nest at all,
But through the wood she strays
Until she finds one snug and warm,
And there her egg she lays.

The sparrow has a nest of hay,
With feathers warmly lined;
The ring-dove's careless nest of sticks
On lofty trees we find.

Rooks build together in a wood,
And often disagree;
The owl will build inside a barn
Or in a hollow tree.

The blackbird's nest of grass and mud
In brush and bank is found;
The lapwing's darkly spotted eggs
Are laid upon the ground.

The magpie's nest is girt with thorns
In leafless trees or hedge;
The wild duck and the water hen
Build by the water's edge.

Birds build their nests from year to year,
According to their kind,
Some very neat and beautiful,
Some easily designed.

UNKNOWN

The Butterfly and
the Kite

Taller than hills or trees,
  A paper kite
Dancing upon the breeze
Looks down to earth and sees
Zig-zagging to and fro
  Far, far below,
A butterfly in flight.

Still soaring haughtily,
  The kite calls down:
'Take a good look at me!
How would you like to be
Dancing above the world,
  Wind-swept and swirled
Over country and town?'

'Not on your terms,' replied
  The butterfly.
'Puffed out with wind and pride,
Can you not see you're tied?
Who wants to be the toy
  Of a stupid boy? —
Better go free than go high!'

RAYMOND WILSON
*(Adapted from a Russian
fable by Krylov)*

Where the Bee Sucks

Where the bee sucks, there suck I:
In a cowslip's bell I lie;
There I couch when owls do cry.
On a bat's back I do fly
After summer merrily.
Merrily, merrily shall I live now
Under the blossom that hangs on the bough.

WILLIAM SHAKESPEARE

The Snare

I hear a sudden cry of pain!
    There is a rabbit in a snare;
Now I hear the cry again,
    But I cannot tell from where.

But I cannot tell from where
    He is calling out for aid;
Crying on the frightened air,
    Making everything afraid.

Making everything afraid,
    Wrinkling up his little face,
As he cries again for aid;
    And I cannot find the place!

And I cannot find the place
  Where his paw is in the snare:
Little one! Oh, little one!
  I am searching everywhere!

JAMES STEPHENS

The Horse

Hast thou given the horse strength? hast thou clothed
  his neck with thunder?
Canst thou make him afraid as a grasshopper? the glory
  of his nostrils is terrible.
He paweth in the valley, and rejoiceth in his strength:
  he goeth on to meet the armed men.
He mocketh at fear, and is not affrighted; neither
  turneth he back from the sword.
The quiver rattleth against him, the glittering spear
  and the shield.
He swalloweth the ground with fierceness and rage;
  neither believeth he that it is the sound of the trumpet.
He saith among the trumpets, Ha, Ha; and he smelleth
  the battle afar off, the thunder of the captains, and the
  shouting.

THE BIBLE (*Book of Job*)

Spring

The crocus sticks her tongue out
Through the dark ground.
Little shells of almond petals
Have fallen around.
And my small dog runs
With panting tongue
Like an almond petal
Rosy and long.
'Spring is here, spring has come,'
Says the thrush's song.

MARGARET STANLEY-WRENCH

Anglo-Saxon Riddle

In former days my mother and father
Forsook me for dead, for the fullness of life
Was not yet within me. But another woman
Graciously fitted me out in soft garments,
As kind to me as to her own children,
Tended and took me under her wing;
Until under her shelter, unlike her kin,
I matured as a mighty bird (as was my fate).
My guardian then fed me until I could fly,
And could wander more widely on my
Excursions; she had the less of her own
Sons and daughters by what she did thus.

Translated by KEVIN CROSSLEY-HOLLAND

(Answer on page 86)

Goblin Market

Morning and evening
Maids heard the goblins cry,
'Come buy our orchard fruits,
Come buy, come buy:
Apples and quinces,
Lemons and oranges,
Plump unpecked cherries,
Melons and raspberries,
Bloom-down-cheeked peaches.
Swart-headed mulberries,
Wild free-born cranberries,
Crab-apples, dewberries,
Pine-apples, blackberries,
Apricots, strawberries; —
All ripe together,
In summer weather, —
Morns that pass by,
Fair eves that fly;
Come buy, come buy;
Our grapes fresh from the vine,
Pomegranates full and fine,
Dates and sharp bullaces,
Rare pears and greengages,
Damsons and bilberries,
Taste them and try:

Currants and gooseberries,
Bright-fire-like barberries,
Figs to fill your mouth,
Citrons from the South,
Sweet to tongue and sound to eye,
Come buy, come buy.'

CHRISTINA ROSSETTI

Autumn

I love the fitful gust that shakes
   The casement all the day,
And from the glossy elm tree takes
   The faded leaves away,
Twirling them by the window pane
   With thousand others down the lane.

I love to see the cottage smoke
   Curl upwards through the trees,
The pigeons nestled round the cote
   On November days like these:
The cock upon the dunghill crowing,
   The mill-sails on the heath a-going.

The feather from the raven's breast
   Falls on the stubble lea,
The acorns near the old crow's nest
   Drop pattering down the tree:
The grunting pigs that wait for all,
   Scramble and hurry where they fall.

JOHN CLARE

Sheep in Winter

The sheep get up and make their many tracks
And bear a load of snow upon their backs,
And gnaw the frozen turnip to the ground
With sharp quick bite, and then go noising round
The boy that pecks the turnips all the day
And knocks his hands to keep the cold away
And laps his legs in straw to keep them warm
And hides behind the hedges from the storm.
The sheep, as tame as dogs, go where he goes
And try to shake their fleeces from the snows,
Then leave their frozen meal and wander round
The stubble stack that stands beside the ground,
And lie all night and face the drizzling storm
And shun the hovel where they might be warm.

JOHN CLARE

The Wind

What way does the Wind come? What way does he go?
He rides over the water, and over the snow,
Through wood and through vale: and o'er rocky height
Which goat cannot climb, takes his sounding flight.
He tosses about in every bare tree,
As, if you look up, you plainly may see;
But how he will come, and whither he goes,
There's never a scholar in England knows.

DOROTHY WORDSWORTH

Trade Winds

In the harbour, in the island, in the Spanish Seas,
Are the tiny white houses and the orange-trees,
And day-long, night-long, the cool pleasant breeze
    Of the steady Trade Winds blowing.

There is the red wine, the nutty Spanish ale,
The shuffle of the dancers, the old salt's tale,
To squeaking fiddle, and the soughing in the sail
    Of the steady Trade Winds blowing.

And o' nights there's fireflies and the yellow moon,
And in the ghostly palm-trees the sleepy tune
Of the quiet voices calling me, the long low croon
    Of the steady Trade Winds blowing.

JOHN MASEFIELD

Gipsy Dance

I saw the gipsy queen
Dancing the flamenco,
Her flowing skirts changing, luminous in the light of
    the fire,
That rough black flowing main twisting.
She jumped,
Oh how she jumped over the bitter roaring fire!

All the gipsy folk,
Their faces black in the shadows,
Waited.
Then, she fell on her knees
As though she were praying to God in the highest.
Oh how the gipsy folk clapped!
They clapped as hard as the moon shone.

LINDA DAVIES (Aged eleven)

The Keys of Heaven

I will give you the keys of heaven,
I will give you the keys of heaven,
Madam, will you walk? Madam, will you talk?
Madam, will you walk and talk with me?

Though you give me the keys of heaven,
Though you give me the keys of heaven,
Yet I will not walk; no, I will not talk;
No, I will not walk or talk with thee.

I will give you a blue silk gown,
To make you fine when you go to town;
Madam, will you walk? Madam, will you talk?
Madam, will you walk and talk with me?

Though you give me a blue silk gown,
To make me fine when I go to town;
Yet I will not walk; no, I will not talk;
No, I will not walk or talk with thee.

I will give you a coach and six,
Six black horses as black as pitch;
Madam, will you walk? Madam, will you talk?
Madam, will you walk and talk with me?

Though you give me a coach and six,
Six black horses as black as pitch;
Yet I will not walk; no, I will not talk;
No, I will not walk or talk with thee.

I will give you the keys of my heart,
And we'll be married till death us do part;
Madam, will you walk? Madam, will you talk?
Madam, will you walk and talk with me?

Thou shalt give me the keys of thy heart,
And we'll be married till death us do part;
I will walk, I will talk;
I will walk and talk with thee.

FOLK SONG

The Waves of the Sea

Don't you go too near the sea,
     The sea is sure to wet you.
Harmless though she seems to be
     The sea's ninth wave will get you!
But I can see the small white waves
     That want to play with me —
They won't do more than wet my feet
     When I go near the sea.

Don't you go too near the sea,
    She does not love a stranger.
Eight untroubled waves has she,
    The ninth is full of danger !
But I can see the smooth blue waves
    That want to play with me —
They won't do more than wet my knees
    When I go near the sea.

Don't you go too near the sea,
    She'll set her waves upon you.
Eight will treat you playfully,
    Until the ninth has won you.
But I can see the big green waves
    That want to play with me —
They won't do more than wet my waist
    When I go near the sea.

Don't you go too near the sea,
    Her ways are full of wonder.
Her first eight waves will leave you free,
    Her ninth will take you under !
But I can see the great grey waves
    That want to play with me —
They won't do more than wet my neck
    When I go near the sea.

Don't you go too near the sea —
　　O Child, you set me quaking!
Eight have passed you silently,
　　And now the ninth is breaking!
I see a wave as high as a wall
　　That wants to play with me —
O Mother, O Mother, it's taken me all,
　　For I went too near the sea!

ELEANOR FARJEON

Nod

Softly along the road of evening,
　　In a twilight dim with rose,
Wrinkled with age, and drenched with dew,
　　Old Nod, the shepherd, goes.

His drowsy flock streams on before him,
　　Their fleeces charged with gold,
To where the sun's last beam leans low
　　On Nod the shepherd's fold.

The hedge is quick and green with briar,
　　From their sand the conies creep;
And all the birds that fly in heaven
　　Flock singing home to sleep.

His lambs outnumber a noon's roses,
　　Yet, when night's shadows fall,
His blind old sheep-dog, Slumber-soon,
　　Misses not one of all.

His are the quiet steeps of dreamland,
    The waters of no-more-pain,
His ram's bell rings 'neath an arch of stars,
    'Rest, rest, and rest again.'

WALTER DE LA MARE

Bird and Beast

Did any bird come flying
After Adam and Eve,
When the door was shut against them,
And they sat down to grieve?

I think not Eve's peacock,
Splendid to see.
And I think not Adam's eagle;
But a dove maybe.

Did any beast come pushing
Through the thorny hedge?
Into the thorny, thistly world,
Out from Eden's edge?

I think not a lion,
Though his strength is such;
But I think an innocent lamb
May have done as much.

CHRISTINA ROSSETTI

One more River

Old Noah once he built the ark,
There's one more river to cross;
And patched it up with hickory bark,
There's one more river to cross.

One more river, and that's the river of Jordan,
One more river, there's one more river to cross.

He went to work to load his stock,
There's one more river to cross;
He anchored the ark with a great big rock,
There's one more river to cross.

The animals went in one by one,
There's one more river to cross;
The elephant chewing a caraway bun,
There's one more river to cross.

The animals went in two by two,
There's one more river to cross;
The rhinoceros and the kangaroo,
There's one more river to cross.

The animals went in three by three,
There's one more river to cross;
The bear, the flea and the bumble bee,
There's one more river to cross.

The animals went in four by four,
There's one more river to cross;
Old Noah got mad and hollered for more,
There's one more river to cross.

The animals went in five by five,
There's one more river to cross;
With Saratoga trunks they did arrive,
There's one more river to cross.

The animals went in six by six,
There's one more river to cross;
The hyena laughed at the monkey's tricks,
There's one more river to cross.

The animals went in seven by seven,
There's one more river to cross;
Said the ant to the elephant, 'Who're you a-shovin'?'
There's one more river to cross.

The animals went in eight by eight,
There's one more river to cross;
They came with a rush 'cause it was so late,
There's one more river to cross.

The animals went in nine by nine,
There's one more river to cross;
Old Noah shouted, 'Cut that line.'
There's one more river to cross.

The animals went in ten by ten,
  There's one more river to cross;
The ark she blew her whistle then,
  There's one more river to cross.

One more river, and that's the river of Jordan,
One more river, there's one more river to cross.

NEGRO SPIRITUAL

Psalm 23

The Lord is my shepherd;
I shall not want.
He maketh me to lie down in green pastures:
He leadeth me beside the still waters.
He restoreth my soul:
He leadeth me in the paths of righteousness
For his name's sake.

Yea, though I walk through the valley of the
    shadow of death,
I will fear no evil:
For thou art with me;
Thy rod and thy staff they comfort me.

Thou preparest a table before me
In the presence of mine enemies:
Thou anointest my head with oil;
My cup runneth over.

Surely goodness and mercy shall follow me
All the days of my life:
And I will dwell in the house of the Lord
For ever.

THE BIBLE

The Birds

When Jesus Christ was four years old,
The angels brought Him toys of gold,
Which no man ever had bought or sold.

And yet with these He would not play.
He made Him small fowl out of clay,
And blessed them till they flew away:
    Tu creasti Domine.

Jesus Christ, Thou child so wise,
Bless mine hands and fill mine eyes,
And bring my soul to Paradise.

HILAIRE BELLOC

The Huron Carol

'Twas in the moon of winter-time,
   When all the birds had fled,
That mighty Gitchi Manitou
   Sent angel choirs instead;

68

Before their light the stars grew dim,
And wandering hunters heard the hymn:
  Jesus your King is born.

Within a lodge of broken bark
  The tender Babe was found,
A ragged robe of rabbit skin
  Enwrapped his beauty round:
But as the hunter braves drew nigh,
The angel-song rang loud and high.
  Jesus your King is born.

The earliest moon of winter-time
  Is not so round and fair
As was the ring of glory on
  The helpless Infant there.
The chiefs from far before him knelt
With gifts of fox and beaver-pelt.
  Jesus your King is born.

O children of the forest free,
  O sons of Manitou,
The Holy Child of earth and heaven
  Is born today for you.
Come kneel before the radiant Boy,
Who brings you beauty, peace and joy.
  Jesus your King is born.

J. EDGAR MIDDLETON
(*Canadian carol, originally French*)

Gitchi Manitou: the supreme God.

69

Kings came Riding

Kings came riding
  One, two, and three,
Over the desert
  And over the sea.

One in a ship
  With a silver mast;
The fishermen wondered
  As he went past.

One on a horse
  With a saddle of gold;
The children came running
  To behold.

One came walking,
  Over the sand,
With a casket of treasure
  Held in his hand.

All the people
  Said, 'Where go they?'
But the kings went forward
  All through the day.

Night came on
  As those kings went by;
They shone like the gleaming
  Stars in the sky.

CHARLES WILLIAMS

In the Town

Joseph	Take heart, the journey's ended:
	I see the twinkling lights,
	Where we shall be befriended
	On this the night of nights.

Mary	Now praise the Lord that led us
	So safe into the town,
	Where men will feed and bed us,
	And I can lay me down.

Joseph	And how then shall we praise him?
	Alas, my heart is sore
	That we no gifts can raise him
	We are so very poor.

Mary	We have as much as any
	That on the earth do live,
	Although we have no penny,
	We have ourselves to give.

Joseph	Look yonder, wife, look yonder!
	A hostelry I see,
	Where travellers that wander
	Will very welcome be.

Mary	The house is tall and stately,
	The door stands open thus;
	Yet, husband, I fear greatly
	That inn is not for us.

Joseph	God save you, gentle master!
	Your littlest room indeed
	With plainest walls of plaster
	Tonight will serve our need.
Host	For lordlings and for ladies
	I've lodging and to spare;
	For you and yonder maid is
	No closet anywhere.
Joseph	Take heart, take heart, sweet Mary,
	Another inn I spy,
	Whose host will not be chary
	To let us easy lie.
Mary	O aid me, I am ailing,
	My strength is nearly gone;
	I feel my limbs are failing,
	And yet we must go on.
Joseph	God save you, Hostess, kindly!
	I pray you, house my wife,
	Who bears beside me blindly
	The burden of her life.
Hostess	My guests are rich men's daughters,
	And sons, I'd have you know!
	Seek out the poorer quarters,
	Where ragged people go.

Joseph	Good sir, my wife's in labour,
	Some corner let us keep.
Host	Not I: knock up my neighbour,
	And as for me, I'll sleep.
Mary	In all the lighted city
	Where rich men welcome win,
	Will not one house for pity
	Take two poor strangers in?
Joseph	Good woman, I implore you,
	Afford my wife a bed.
Hostess	Nay, nay, I've nothing for you
	Except the cattle shed.
Mary	Then gladly in the manger
	Our bodies we will house,
	Since men tonight are stranger
	Than asses are and cows.
Joseph	Take heart, take heart, sweet Mary,
	The cattle are our friends,
	Lie down, lie down, sweet Mary,
	For here our journey ends.
Mary	Now praise the Lord that found me
	This shelter in the town,
	Where I with friends around me
	May lay my burden down.

UNKNOWN

74

All in the Morning

It was on Christmas Day,
  And all in the morning,
Our Saviour was born
  And our heavenly King:
    And was not this a joyful thing?
    And sweet Jesus they called him by name.

It was on the Twelfth Day,
  And all in the morning,
The Wise Men were led
  To our heavenly King:
    And was not this a joyful thing?
    And sweet Jesus they called him by name.

It was on Holy Wednesday,
  And all in the morning,
That Judas betrayed
  Our dear heavenly King:
    And was not this a woeful thing?
    And sweet Jesus we'll call him by name.

It was on Good Friday,
  And all in the morning,
They crucified our Saviour,
  And our heavenly King:
    And was not this a woeful thing?
    And sweet Jesus we'll call him by name.

It was on Easter Day,
    And all in the morning,
Our Saviour arose,
    Our own heavenly King:
        The sun and the moon they did both rise with
            him,
        And sweet Jesus we'll call him by name.

CAROL

The Twelve Days
of Christmas

On the first day of Christmas
My true love sent to me
A partridge in a pear-tree.

On the second day of Christmas
My true love sent to me
Two turtle-doves, and
A partridge in a pear-tree.

On the third day of Christmas
My true love sent to me
Three French hens,
Two turtle-doves, and
A partridge in a pear-tree.

On the fourth day of Christmas
My true love sent to me
Four colly birds,
Three French hens,
Two turtle-doves, and
A partridge in a pear-tree.

On the fifth day of Christmas
My true love sent to me
Five gold rings,
Four colly birds,
Three French hens,
Two turtle-doves, and
A partridge in a pear-tree.

On the sixth day of Christmas
My true love sent to me
Six geese a-laying,
Five gold rings,
Four colly birds,
Three French hens,
Two turtle-doves, and
A partridge in a pear-tree.

On the seventh day of Christmas
My true love sent to me
Seven swans a-swimming,
Six geese a-laying,
Five gold rings,

Four colly birds,
Three French hens,
Two turtle-doves, and
A partridge in a pear-tree.

On the eighth day of Christmas
My true love sent to me
Eight maids a-milking,
Seven swans a-swimming,
Six geese a-laying,
Five gold rings,
Four colly birds,
Three French hens,
Two turtle-doves, and
A partridge in a pear-tree.

On the ninth day of Christmas
My true love sent to me
Nine drummers drumming,
Eight maids a-milking,
Seven swans a-swimming,
Six geese a-laying,
Five gold rings,
Four colly birds,
Three French hens,
Two turtle-doves, and
A partridge in a pear-tree.

On the tenth day of Christmas
My true love sent to me
Ten pipers piping,
Nine drummers drumming,
Eight maids a-milking,
Seven swans a-swimming,
Six geese a-laying,
Five gold rings,
Four colly birds,
Three French hens,
Two turtle-doves, and
A partridge in a pear-tree.

On the eleventh day of Christmas
My true love sent to me
Eleven ladies dancing,
Ten pipers piping,
Nine drummers drumming,
Eight maids a-milking,
Seven swans a-swimming,
Six geese a-laying,
Five gold rings,
Four colly birds,
Three French hens,
Two turtle-doves, and
A partridge in a pear-tree.

On the twelfth day of Christmas
My true love sent to me
Twelve lords a-leaping,
Eleven ladies dancing,
Ten pipers piping,
Nine drummers drumming,
Eight maids a-milking,
Seven swans a-swimming,
Six geese a-laying,
Five gold rings,
Four colly birds,
Three French hens,
Two turtle-doves, and
A partridge in a pear-tree.

UNKNOWN

Hushed was
the Evening Hymn

Hushed was the evening hymn,
　The temple courts were dark,
The lamp was burning dim
　Before the sacred ark,
When suddenly a voice divine
Rang through the silence of the shrine.

The old man, meek and mild,
 The priest of Israel, slept;
His watch the temple child,
 The little Levite, kept:
And what from Eli's sense was sealed
The Lord to Hannah's son revealed.

O give me Samuel's ear,
 The open ear, O Lord,
Alive and quick to hear
 Each whisper of Thy word,
Like him to answer at Thy call,
And to obey Thee first of all.

O give me Samuel's heart,
 A lowly heart that waits
Where in Thy house Thou art,
 Or watches at Thy gates
By day and night — a heart that still
Moves at the breathing of Thy will.

O give me Samuel's mind,
 A sweet unmurmuring faith,
Obedient and resigned
 To Thee in life and death,
That I may read with childlike eyes
Truths that are hidden from the wise.

JAMES DRUMMOND BURNS

Glory to Thee

Glory to Thee, my God, this night,
For all the blessings of the light:
Keep me, O keep me, King of kings,
Beneath Thine own almighty wings.

O may my soul on Thee repose,
And may sweet sleep mine eyelids close,
Sleep that shall me more vigorous make
To serve my God when I awake.

If in the night I sleepless lie,
My soul with heavenly thoughts supply;
Let no ill dreams disturb my rest,
No powers of darkness me molest.

All praise to Thee in light arrayed,
Who light Thy dwelling-place hast made;
A boundless ocean of bright beams
From Thy all-glorious Godhead streams.

Praise God, from whom all blessings flow,
Praise Him, all creatures here below;
Praise Him above, ye heavenly host:
Praise Father, Son and Holy Ghost.

T. KEN

Index of Authors

Index of First Lines

Answer to riddle on page 55: a cuckoo